MEET MEAT

BY

SNAPP AND REDDEN

ILLUSTRATED BY

JUST ANOTHER GUILD

**DreamLoud Publishing
dreamloudkids.com**

Copyright © 2021

All rights reserved. No part of this book may be reproduced, stored in retrieval system, or transmitted in any form or by any means, electronic, mechanical, photocopying, recording, or otherwise without the written permission of DreamLoud Publishing.

Printed in the United States of America

Dedicated to our Mom, with love

Have you heard about how one great big cow
jumped over the monster moon?
Well here's a tale I'd love to tell
'bout a cow I met last June.

Let's meet Meat (she's really quite sweet),
and focus on her alone.
She's a dairy cow, but you'll soon see how
she became so really well-known.

Meat's skin was green (which I'd never seen
on a cow with blackish spots).
She cheered her peers throughout the year
and was known for positive thoughts.

She encouraged the rest to be their best,
her trough a half-pail full.
She always blessed each farmhouse guest,
even called the fool bulls "Cool!"

But there was a day when Meat would say
her light grew pretty dim.
She was feeling blue because Farmer Drew
sought to sell her on a whim.

To make it worse, O what a curse!
Meat heard these words from the mice:
"At the end of week, Drew will seek
the BUTCHER's asking price!"

Now it may seem sad or make you mad
that Drew would sell his cow;
It happens a lot, and so Drew thought,
"Meat's meat will buy my plow."

She couldn't hide, so poor Meat tried
to show her other skills,
But Drew was firm, at the end of the term,
he'd seal the dreaded deal.

Wrong or right, Meat couldn't fight,
She worried all the day.
Her upbeat cheer replaced by tears,
her green skin turned to gray.

Full of stress and so depressed,
Meat wandered all alone.
Her nervous shakes kept her awake
and turned her milk to foam.

She asked advice of the wisest mice,
"What will be my fate?"
"How can I run from burger buns
and avoid the barbecue plates?"

"I don't want to die," Meat cried with a sigh,
"I'm young and in my prime."
"I don't have a clue what I can do,
and I'm almost out of time!"

Scratching their heads, "Pray!" they said,
and Meat thought that was smart.
So she bowed her head and prayed instead
to the God who knew her heart.

And with the light came new insight,
"I'll choose to cling to hope!"
"I'll live without fear, like 'Cow of the Year,'
though Drew should bring his rope."

And it was on her way to the end of her days,
Drew leading her down Main,
Meat saw her chance to stay in the dance
and earn her current fame!

Drew suffered from thirst, so he stopped in first
to Steerbucks for a chai.
Meat marched right in, determined to win,
bowed to the crowd and cried:

"I'm Marvelous Meat, so have a seat.
Here's service with a moo!"
"From caramel cream to vanilla bean,
I'm a One-Cow-Café-Crew!"

Defying the rules of cows and bulls,
she rushed behind the counter.
The baristas stood like blocks of wood,
though shocked, they couldn't doubt her.

A smile on her face and apron in place,
Meat started filling up glasses.
Standing upright, she set her sights
on pleasing thirsty masses.

From one to another, with a flick of her udders,
she served every customer's wish.
From Grande to Tall, she filled them all,
while her tail waved a happy "Swish!"

From left milker 1, like the shot from a gun,
she produced a mocha latte.
From right milker 2, with a shout, "Moo-hoo!"
She poured a vanilla frappe.

"Espresso shot? Why not?" she thought,
"it seems that along with my cream,
I'm uniquely created by the God of the ages
to generate loads of caffeine!"

The customers gawked and the owner squawked,
"This cow's a golden goose!"
"She'll make me a ton and be lots of fun,
I'd be crazy to turn this cow loose!"

He ran to Drew, who was wide-eyed too—
His arm around Drew's neck,
"Let's settle this now, you can buy 3 plows,"
and he offered a generous check.

Drew was elated and the crowd celebrated.
It seemed that his cow was a hit.
When he doubled Meat's fee, the owner agreed!
Meat cried when she heard of it.

Dancing and twirling, her black spots a-whirling,
Meat was full of surprises.
She concocted new drinks with a snort and a wink,
Cow-puccinos in all sorts of sizes!

She avoided the knife and thus saved her life
by refusing to believe the world's lies.
With talents galore, she knew she had more,
so she seized on her chance to arise.

"Though I may be a cow, don't assume that somehow
I'm exactly like all the others.
I'm more than a steak that you grill or you bake
or the source for your milk and your butter."

"I'm Meat, and I'm neat and I'd like to repeat,
I'm a one-of-a-kind kind of cow!"
"I'm special indeed, a spectacular breed—
a bovine brand of 'Wow!'"

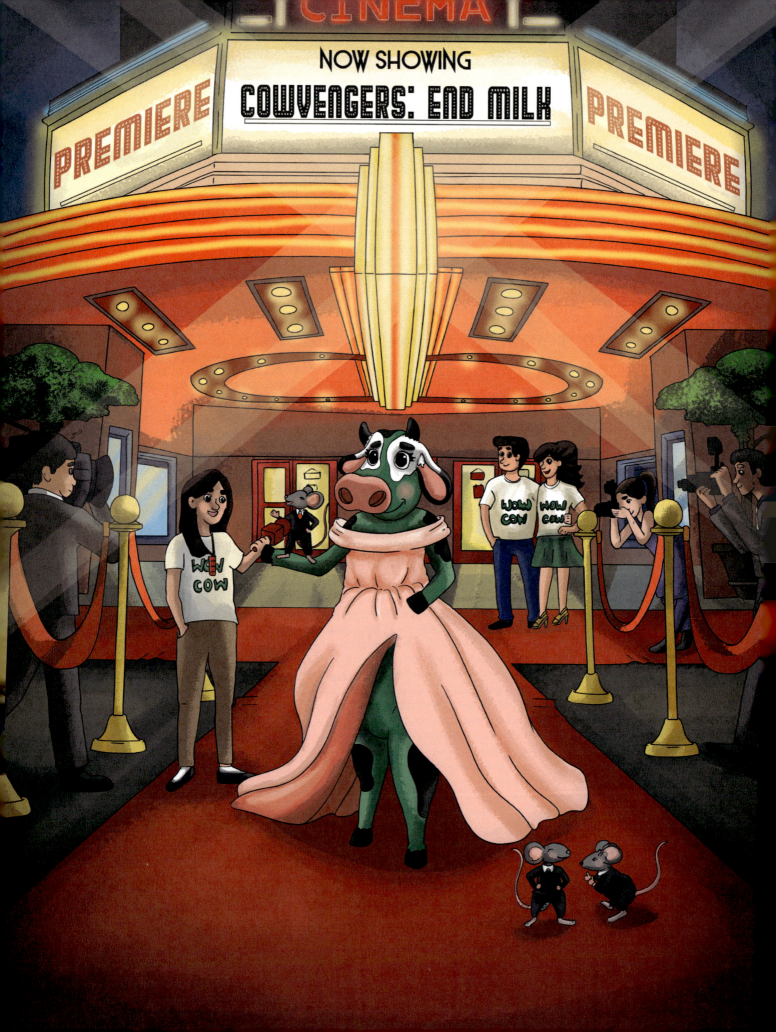

So, what about YOU is uniquely "Moo-hoo?"
Are you fighting some false expectations?
Though the crowds may be loud, don't ever allow
them to cage you with their regulations.

It's never too late to alter your fate
by opening blinded eyes.
You were made for a cause that will bring much applause,
like Meat you're a wonderful prize!

How are you wired? What makes you inspired?
Be bold and determined to win it!
Work hard every day and train the same way,
and maximize each extra minute!

Let God give you hope when you're faced with a rope.
Trust Him to open the door.
Then prepare to mooooove out with a victory shout.
Believe you were made for much more!

About the Authors

Snapp & Redden are brothers from West Texas who love to laugh and make others smile with their offbeat humor. They are dedicated to entertaining, encouraging and challenging children of all ages to rise above the obstacles, false expectations, and lies that assault them on a regular basis. The author's funny, memorable, and often zany outlook, along with their amusing poetic style, are sure to resonate with young and "still feeling young" readers and listeners. The stories give parents an enjoyable teaching platform with which to discuss difficult issues—and if parents aren't careful, they just might learn something, too!

Meet Meat is their first story to be released but watch for more titles like Dean the Bean Gets a Screen, Tarke the Shark, and a myriad of other heroes they have created for your enjoyment.

If you like the books and want to encourage Snapp & Redden to keep producing, please tell your friends and leave a positive comment with a 5-star rating.

If you'd like to contact them with feedback or ideas for new stories, you can do so through the publishers at DreamLoud Kids via email or Instagram.